Table of Contents

What Are Bees? 4
Facts About Bees 6
Options for treating bee stings 7
The Life Cycle of a Bee 8
Why Are Bees So Important to Humans? 11
Types of Bees 12
Bumble Bees 15
Yellow Jackets 16
Wasps 17
The Bee Hive 18
The Honey Bee Colony 20
The Royal Queen 22
Bee Keeping 24
Tips for Preventing Attacks 26
Harvesting Honey 29
What is Pollen and Pollination? 31
Flowers That Attract Bees 34
Publisher 38
Credits of Photography 44

What Are Bees?

Bees are referred to as flying insects, closely related to ants and wasps. There are over 19,000 known species of bees. Bees are made up of three body parts, the head, thorax, and abdomen. The head is at the top of the body containing:

1. The antenna.
2. Two compound eyes made up of thousands of tiny lenses.
3. Three other eyes called simple eyes or O eyes.

The bee also has a mouth! The bees' mouth is made up of:

1. The paired mandibles, like our jaw.
2. The glassa, like our tongue..
3. The labrum and maxillae, which are like our lips, support the proboscis, or "tube" for collecting nectar!

The thorax is the smaller middle section of the body containing:

1. Three pair of legs with hooks on the ends so that they may easily cling on to objects.
2. Four clear wings, they flap their wings up to 11,400 times a minute and that is where the buzzing sound comes from!

The abdomen is the lower and largest part of the body that has a nectar pouch and stomach the end of the abdomen contains the stinger! Ouch!

Facts About Bees

1. A honey bee is not born knowing how to make honey, they are taught by more experienced bees.
2. A honey bee will make only 1/12 of a teaspoon of honey in its lifetime.
3. Are the only insects that produce food eaten by humans.
4. Honey bees must consume 16-18 pounds of honey to make each pound of beeswax.
5. Bees have been around 30 million years.
6. Over 1000 bee stings are considered to be fatal.
7. Honey bees are not native to the Americas.
8. Bees are cold blooded.
9. Bacteria cannot grow in honey because of the natural preservatives.
10. Bears prefer to eat the bee larvae rather than the honey.
11. Bees communicate through smells and dances.
12. Bees can fly up to 15 miles per hour.
13. A hive will fly almost 100,000 miles to collect 1kg of honey.
14. It would only take one ounce of honey to feed a bee and if possible give them enough energy to fly all the way around the world.

Options for treating bee stings

After a sting the first step is always to remove the stinger and wash the site. Make sure an allergic reaction that requires emergency services is not happening. The next step is up to you, there are many methods to treating a bee or wasp sting to minimize the pain.
1. Apply ice for 20 minutes.
2. Apply toothpaste for 15 minutes.
3. Apply wet tobacco for 15 minutes.
4. Make a paste out of baking soda, vinegar and meat tenderizer, apply for 20 minutes.
5. Apply calamine lotion
6. Apply hydrocortisone cream.
7. Apply honey for 30 minutes.
8. Rub a stick across the site.

Some of the natural remedies to treat bee stings might sound silly but they have been proven to at least slightly reduce the symptoms of a sting.

Bees are amazing, intelligent, and beneficial insects to the world. They are beautiful and serve many purposes, our way of life would be much different if it wasn't for the tiny insects that we call bees. Remember, that they do us more good than they do harm and are a beautiful part of nature that we get to enjoy in more ways than one!

The Life Cycle of a Bee

There are four different stages of a bees' life cycle.
1. Egg
2. Larvae
3. Pupa

4. Adult

Stage 1: The queen lays soft white eggs inside the comb. The egg stays an egg for 3 days.

Stage 2: On the third day, the larvae turns into pupa. It now has eyes, wings, and legs.

Stage 3: This is the final stage in a bees' metamorphosis. It is now fully grown. The bee will chew its way out of the cell. It becomes an adult on days 16-24.

After the adult bee emerges from the cell it has a specific job for its age throughout its life until death.

Days:

1-2 the bee will clean the cells and keep the brood nest warm.

3-5 the bee will feed the older larvae honey and pollen.

6-11 the bee will feed the young larvae with royal jelly.

12-16 the bee will produce wax and construct comb, as well as ripen honey.

16-20 the bee will guard the hive entrance and help circulate air to the hive.

21-death the bee will forage for nectar, pollen, propolis, and water.

The life of a bee is very hard work!

Why Are Bees So Important to Humans?

Bees are important to humans because of pollination. Our agriculture depends on honey bees for this. 80% of all insect pollination is done by honey bees. Without this pollination we would have a substantial decrease in the amount of fruits and vegetables being grown. Bees can visit more than 2 million flowers a year, and collect 66 pounds of pollen, per year, per hive, that is a lot of pollen!

Types of Bees

There are about 25,000 species of bees in the world. These 25,000 species can be divided into over 400 types of bees, belonging to 9 families, all under the same super family-'Apoidea'. I will share a few details about the most common types of bees that humans are familiar with.

Carpenter bees

Carpenter bees are large bees found throughout the world. There are 500 species of carpenter bees. Their name comes from the fact that they all build their nests in burrows inside of wood! They make their nests by vibrating their mandibles against the wood, resulting in tunnels. They are likely to live alone or, occasionally in a small group of females. The females will split up the work load having specific chores quite like the honey bee! Carpenter bees can be pollinators to open faced flowers although they are also known to "steal" nectar, by slitting the side of the sides of the flowers.
 Stealing the nectar, means that they are not pollenating at all by their eating. Carpenter bees can be mistaken for bumblebees because they are similar in size and color. The way to tell the difference in carpenter bees and bumble bees is that carpenter bees have a shiny abdomen and bumble bees have a hairy abdomen. Male carpenters sometimes have a yellow or white face, while females do not. Males

also have much larger eyes than females and no stinger. Female carpenter bees are docile and usually will not sting unless they are caught in the hand or provoked in some way.

Africanized honey bees

Africanized bees are known to us by the ever dramatic name "killer bees". They got their name "killer" bees because they will viciously attack people or animals that come upon their territory. The Africanized honey bee colony does not have to be provoked like other types of bees to trigger an attack, they are quicker to swarm, and can attack in great numbers. They will also attack a great distance away from their hive. They stay agitated longer than regular honey bees, and will fly a great distance to attack their victim. They like to develop their hives near drainage ditches and canals, because they like to be near water, so look out for bee hives when you are near water, as it could possibly be an African honey bee hive. Watch for swarms of bees when it looks like it is about to rain, African honey bees swarm when they sense rain. Africanized honey bees are a result of honey bees brought from Africa to Brazil in the 1950's so that scientist could try to develop a honey bee that was better adapted to live in tropical areas. Eventually they spread north and south and reached the United States in October of 1990. Africanized honey bees can be found in most of southern Texas, New Mexico, California and all over Arizona. They will continue to migrate north.

Bumble Bees

Bumble bees are yellow and black furry bees that you may often see fly around your garden during summer. They spend most of their time pollenating plants and gathering nectar to make honey, although they do not make anywhere near the same amount of honey as honey bees do. Bumble bees will only sting when provoked. Instead of a hive, like a honey bee, a bumble bee prefers to make its nest in soft spots, like piles of leaves or in cushions of patio furniture. Bumble bees are very large and beautiful bees.

Yellow Jackets

Yellow jackets get their names from the fact that they have very bright yellow and black stripes, these are very easy to spot and differentiate from others. Yellow jackets are attracted to sweet things like ice cream and lemonade, if you are out on a summer day with a sweet treat you are sure to spot a few buzzing yellow jackets. They produce a paper like substance by chewing little pieces of wood. This is what they make their nest out of, you are likely to find these hanging from your roof, deck, attic, or in trees. Another type of yellow jacket is the ground bee type which makes their nest in abandoned mouse holes or mole holes, you will want to watch out for these when you are mowing the lawn, they can get quite angry when disturbed!

Wasps

Wasps are very beneficial to humans by controlling pest insect populations. The wasps eat these pest or use them as a host for its parasitic larvae. Wasps are so good at controlling pest populations that the agriculture industry regularly deploys them to protect crops. Wasps are distinguishable from other bees because of their very narrow midsection that separates the abdomen from the thorax. They come in many different colors from yellow to brown or red. It would be very unfortunate however, to stumble across a wasps nest, they are likely to swarm and sting repeatedly. If you ever spot a wasp, it would be smart to steer clear!

The Bee Hive

A bee hive is the house or nest that the bees make to live in and it is one of the worlds' most efficient facilities! Hives are usually made in a hollow tree, branch or in the crevice of a rock. When a colony of bees are looking for a new home, they send out "scouts" to find a new location. These scouts can fly 55 miles or more away from their original hive and always find their way back, to lead the rest of the bees to their new location. At their new home, the bees will chew up honey that they have brought with them from the last hive until it is soft and becomes beeswax.

Beeswax is used to build many honeycombs which are made to store honey, pollen, nectar and to house the bees, and give the queen a place to lay her eggs. After many honey combs are built, the bees collect something called propolis from trees. The propolis is actually tree resin and it is used to coat the outside of the honeycomb so that it becomes enclosed to protect it from predators. A circular entrance to the hive is made near the bottom and a few young worker bees will stand guard to watch for danger! Most hives are built in the shape of a dome. Inside the dome, the honey is stored in the upper most part, then there are rows of pollen storage cells, then the worker brood cells, and then drone brood cells. The queen lives in the lower most part of the hive.

The bees squeeze in very close together to keep the hive at a warm, constant temperature of 86-95 degrees. This is just the right temperature for producing honey and young bees. A healthy hive in the summer time can have up to 80,000 bees!

The Honey Bee Colony

Bees are very social animals that live in a very well organized colony and have specific jobs. Bees depend on one another and could not survive if they lived on their own. There are three different types of bees that live inside the colony.

1. **The queen bee**: There is only one queen, she is the heart and soul of the bee colony, without her there wouldn't even be a colony because she is the one who lays all of the eggs that hatch into young bees. Her job is to eat as much royal jelly as she can, which makes her fertile to mate with drone bees and lay the eggs. The queen can live from 3-5 years! That is longer than any other bee!

2. **Worker bees:** there are anywhere from 30,000 to 70,000 worker bees in a colony. They all work cooperatively with each other to find food and communicate with each other using a pattern of movement that is called "dancing". Worker bees are very important, these are the bees that do all of the work, hence the name, worker bee! They go back and forth in and out of the hive to flowers and collect pollen and nectar. They perform many different tasks to insure that the colony runs successfully during their short lives of only about 45 days. A worker bees duties include, feeding the queen,

grooming the queen, cleaning the hive, guarding the hive, and circulating air throughout the hive by flapping their wings. Worker bees are all female but cannot reproduce. Worker bees do have a stinger but die shortly after they have stung.

3. **Drones:** drones are male bees there are only around 300-3000 drones in each hive. Drones do not have a stinger and are only used as a reproductive tool for the queen. Drones are of no use to the colony in the winter, so they are expelled from the hive during the autumn.

The Royal Queen

The queen is picked when she is only still a larvae. From that time she is fed a "royal diet" of a substance called "royal jelly". Royal jelly is a milky substance made up of digested pollen, nectar and a chemical secreted from the gland in the nursing bees head. This jelly is what turns a regular bee into a queen bee by making her fertile and able to reproduce. The queen is the largest bee in her colony due to this diet and she is the only one with an almond shaped abdomen. The queen can lay from 2,000 to 3,000 eggs a day, which is more than her own body weight! The queens' only job is to go from cell to cell laying her eggs. This gives her no time to tend to her own needs which is why she has "royal attendants". From the time the queen is just a larvae she is fed and groomed by a worker bee. The queen bee does not ever get to leave the hive during her lifespan, not even to go to the bathroom, a worker bee, removes her waste for her. The queen also regulates the hive by producing a pheromone that guides the behavior of the other bees.

Bee Keeping

If you decide to become a bee keeper, there are a few things you will need in order to make your hive. You can purchase a precut hive frame, or you can build your own hive boxes. If you build your own hive box, you will need to order the instructions or building plan! The color of the outside of the box is important; it needs to be a light color so the hive does not over heat during the summer!

Next, you will need to add bees to your box! You can buy worker bees and have them delivered by mail. The best time to start beekeeping is at the end of spring, so you will want to wait until then to have your bees delivered. You will need to choose your queen very carefully as you are shopping. You will need to find a queen that is bred for "hygienic behavior" which is a genetic trait and means that her worker bees will have superior abilities to clean out larvae with diseases or mites, which can destroy your hive if left in place. For your hive you will need three pounds of bees and a queen, this is around 12,000 bees! Oh my! Once your bees' are inside the box, and you have it painted a light color to keep it cool, you will need to look in every now and then to see what's going on in there! You will need to make sure the colony is running properly, eggs are being laid, and look for any signs of disease.

You will also want to feed your bees some sweet sugar water to supplement nectar.

Hiving your bees can be very scary at first, so make sure that you are completely covered, and zipped up in a bee suit! When working with your hive, try to remain extremely calm, this will help your bees remain calm as well. You will need to make very fluid and slow movements as not to upset the bees. Most bee keepers use a smoker to put out a leafy or pine needle smell that masks the bee's alert pheromone, keeping them somewhat calm. Your bees may want to crawl on your suit! This is quite normal and should not alarm you, bees very seldom sting if they do not feel threatened, by using all of the above methods your bees should not feel that they are in any danger by your presence.

Tips for Preventing Attacks

Tips for preventing attacks:

1. Check around your house and surrounding building and trees for bee colonies.

2. Keep pets and children inside while doing yard work, which could agitate bees.
3. Cover your chimney when not in use.
4. Take notice when you see a few bees to see if there is a colony near by .
5. Have an escape plan.
6. Wear light colored clothing.
7. Do not wear floral scented perfume while doing yard work.
8. Do not try to remove bee hives without professional help.

When an attack happens:

1. Quickly get into a house, car, or some other type of enclosure and close doors and windows.
2. Do not jump in a pool, the bees will wait until you surface to attack.
3. Run away very quickly, do not stop.
4. Protect your face, because bee stings on the face and head are much more dangerous than those on the body, cover your head with your shirt if that is your only source of protection.

Harvesting Honey

It is easiest on your bees to harvest the honey leaving the honey comb intact. They have to ingest six pounds of honey to make one pound of wax, and it is hard work to make the comb! You can buy an electric extractor that will quickly spin the honey from the comb using centrifugal force. Electric extractors are very expensive, you can also join a bee club, where they share an electric extractor and the cost is much lower. Bee clubs often organize honey harvesting parties!

If you do decide to harvest your comb as well you would be able to sell it so that the beeswax could be used in candles, soaps, lotions and other products.

Honey

You can sell your honey as well. Honey is a very tasty food that can be used to sweeten tea, and coffee, or eaten on toast and lots of other foods! Yum! Honey is often bought for health reasons as it is known to reduce allergies if the honey that is taken in is from a local hive. Honey is a very nutritious food containing:

1. Trace enzymes
2. Minerals
3. Vitamins
4. And amino acids!

Honey is the only food that contains all of the substances necessary to sustain life. It is the only food that contains "pinocembrin" which is an antioxidant known to improve brain function.

The specific taste and color of the honey depend on which type of blossom the bee got the nectar from. There are more than 300 different kinds of honey in the United States. Darker honey is usually more robust in flavor and lighter honey are usually light in flavor. I like light honey the best, do you have a favorite kind?

What is Pollen and Pollination?

Pollen is the male germ cells produced by all flowering plants for fertilization and plant embryo formation.

Pollination leads to the creation of new seeds that grow into new plants. Flowering plants have male parts called stamen that produce a sticky substance called pollen. Flowers also have a female part called a pistil, at the top of the pistil is the stigma, which is sticky. Seeds are made at the base of the pistil in the ovule. Pollination happens by the pollen being moved from a stamen to the stigma. This usually happens from animals, insects or the wind.

Animals such as bees, flies, butterflies, moths and birds often pollenate plants when they are getting food such as nectar and pollen from the plant. While they are eating they rub against the stamens and get pollen stuck to them.

When they move on to eat from another plant, they then get the pollen that is stuck to them on the next plants stigma, causing the next plant to become pollinated and so on and so forth. Plants that are pollenated by animals and insects are commonly very colorful and have a strong smell that attracts them! The plants that are pollenated by wind have long stamens and pistils, which makes it easy for the pollen to be blown from stamen to stigma. Plants that are pollenated by the wind can be more dull in color, unscented and have very small or no petals because they do not need insects to land on them for the pollination process!

Flowers That Attract Bees

If you are trying to grow a thriving garden, you will want to attract as many bees as possible, because many plants and vegetables require pollination. You will want to ask your local nursery worker to find out which plants thrive best in your location. Bees are after two things when visiting your plants, pollen, which provides a balanced diet of protein and fats, and nectar that is loaded with sugar and is the bees' main source of energy! First you will want to use native plants, because they are four times more likely to attract native bees to your area than exotic plants. You will want to plant a ground cover of herbs, bees really like herbs such as:

1. Thyme
2. Creeping mint
3. Basil

Flower colors that particularly attract bees are blue, purple, violet, white and yellow!
You will want to plant the flowers in clusters to attract the most bees. There are four thousand different species of bees in North America so you will want to plant as many shapes and sizes of flowers as possible to attract a variety of bees. Some tried and true types of flowers that attract bees are:

1. Annuals
2. Asters
3. Calliopsis
4. Clover
5. Marigolds
6. Sunflowers
7. Buttercups

8. Dahlias
9. Cosmos
10. Crocuses
    Foxglove
11. English ivy
12. Geraniums
13. Germander
14. Globe thistle
15. Hollyhocks
16. Hyacinth
17. Rock cress
18. Roses
19. Sedum
20. Snowdrops
21. Squills
22. And Tansy!

There are many more types of flowers that attract bees as well, just remember that they will need to have a strong scent, a dark color, and supply a good amount of pollen and nectar. Some vegetable plants that attract bees are:

1. Blackberries
2. Cantaloupe
3. Cucumbers
4. Gourds

5. Fruit trees
6. Peppers
7. Pumpkins
8. Raspberries
9. Squash
10. Strawberries

Download Free Books!
http://MendonCottageBooks.com

Publisher

JD-Biz Corp

P O Box 374

Mendon, Utah 84325

http://www.jd-biz.com/

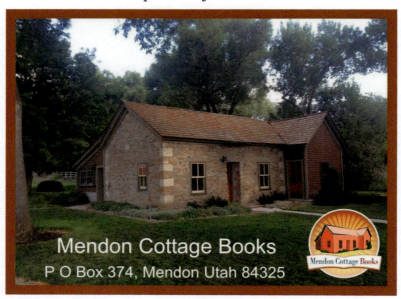

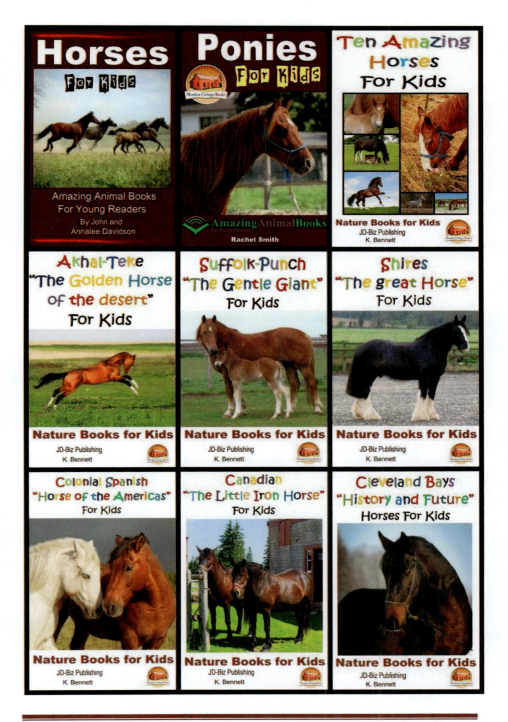

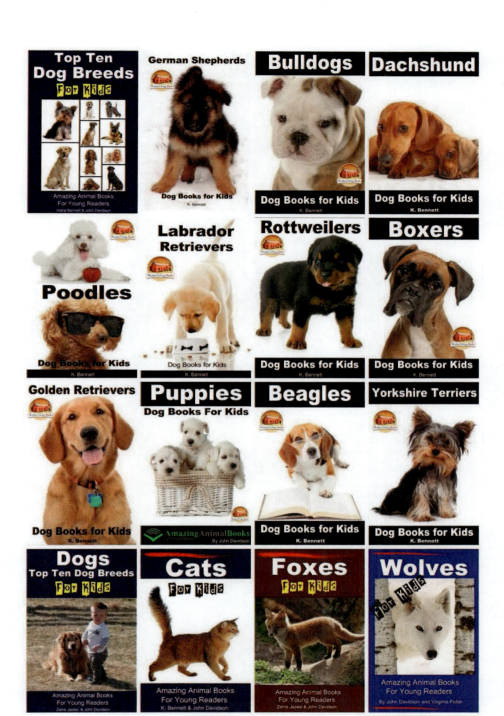

Bees for Kids Page 41

Bees for Kids
Page 42

Bees for Kids　　　　　　　　　　　　　　　　　　　　　　　　　　　Page 43

Download Free Books!
http://MendonCottageBooks.com

Credits of Photography

All Images Licensed by Fotolia.com
worker bee collects pollen from yellow spring broccoli flow
© sherjaca - Fotolia.com
beehives
© S_E - Fotolia.com
Bees on Red Flower
© Lenzcaster - Fotolia.com
A swarm of Thailand honey bees clinging to a tree
© peht - Fotolia.com
bees in hand
© mjwallace - Fotolia.com
miel
© guy - Fotolia.com
bees in the hive
© lnzyx - Fotolia.com
Drop of honey and bees
© The physicist - Fotolia.com
Little boy holding jar of honey
© auremar - Fotolia.com
Western Honey Bee (Apis mellifera)
© waymoreawesomer - Fotolia.com
Honigbiene
© Carola Schubbel - Fotolia.com
Beekeepers 8
© Valeriy Kirsanov - Fotolia.com
Insekten Hotel
© Otmar Smit - Fotolia.com
frelon sur rocher
© skampixel - Fotolia.com
Récupération d'essaim
© Adrien Roussel - Fotolia.com
busy bee
© Wendi Evans - Fotolia.com

bumblebee
© Henryk Olszewski - Fotolia.com
One bee works on honeycomb
© Dmytro Smaglov - Fotolia.com
Botanisches
© nadinsche - Fotolia.com

Bees
For Kids
Amazing Animal Books for Young Readers

by Jennifer Lejeune

Mendon Cottage Books

JD-Biz Publishing

Download Free Books!
http://MendonCottageBooks.com

All Rights Reserved.
No part of this publication may be reproduced in any form or by any means, including scanning, photocopying, or otherwise without prior written permission from JD-Biz Corp and http://AmazingAnimalBooks.com. Copyright © 2015

All Images Licensed by Fotolia and 123RF

Read More Amazing Animal Books

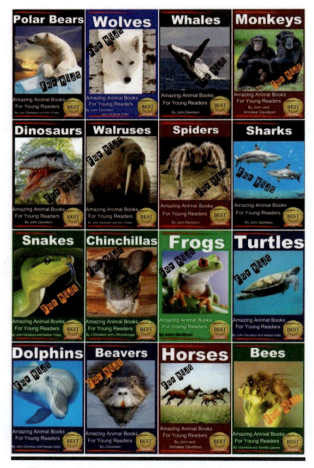

Purchase at Amazon.com